PLAYING

SINGING

STANDING

THINKING

LAUGHING

EATING

DANCING

RUNNING

DRINKING

WATCHING

CRYING

READING

FIGHTING

CYCLING

WINNING

SITTING

SLEEPING

WRITING

JUMPING

WALKING

SMILING

COOKING

WASHING

DEAR READER, YOUR OPINION MATTERS TO US. COULD YOU PLEASE TAKE 1 MINUTE TO LEAVE US AN HONEST REVIEW ON THIS BOOK PAGE. WE APPRECIATE YOUR HELP! THANK YOU.

Printed in Great Britain
by Amazon